To the Wreakers of Havoc

To the Wreakers of Havoc

POEMS BY

MICHAEL HEFFERNAN

The University of Georgia Press
Athens

Published by the University of Georgia Press
Athens, Georgia 30602

Set in 10 on 13 Linotron 202 Palatino
Printed in the United States of America

The paper in this book meets the guidelines for
permanence and durability of the Committee on
Production Guidelines for Book Longevity of the Council
on Library Resources.

Library of Congress Cataloging in Publication Data

Heffernan, Michael.
  To the wreakers of havoc.

  I. Title.
PS3558.E413T6 1984   811'.54   83-9276
ISBN 0-8203-0698-3
ISBN 0-8203-0699-1 (pbk. : alk. paper)

The publication of this book is supported by a grant from
the National Endowment for the Arts, a federal agency.

THIS BOOK IS FOR MY SISTER.

Acknowledgments

The author thanks the editors of the following publications in which poems from this book first appeared, often in earlier versions: *The American Poetry Review:* "Fathers," "The Spring of '64," "The Voice in the Rafters," "The Windowsill" (1, 2, 5, and 6); *Argo:* "The Parting Glass"; *Barnwood:* "Grandmother"; *Carolina Quarterly:* "Afternoon with Angels," "Kathy Dancing"; *The Chowder Review:* "Dreaming of Women," "The Last Great Lover," "The Lives of the Just," "On Completing My 40th Year," "A Tale of Bears and the Blackbirds," "To Cathleen at Patricktide," "The Way West"; *Confluence: Kansas Poetry Anthology:* "The Miracle of the Nails"; *Epoch:* "The Minotaur"; *Kansas Quarterly:* "A Feast in February," "Of Those Dear to Him"; *Memphis State Review:* "The Blessing of the Bones," "The Garden Party," "To the Wreakers of Havoc"; *The Midwest Quarterly:* "Jacob Limps Home over the River," "Pilgrimage," "The Sea off Flanders," "A Voyage to the Island"; *The Morning Sun* (Pittsburg, Kans.): "The Perfect Fool"; *The New American Review:* "Fourteen Sentences at Midwinter," "Midsummer Light as the Soul's Habitat," "A Winter Walk"; *New England Review:* "Brown Socks"; *New Letters:* "For an Epiphany," "Gifts"; *Other Islands:* "The Eighth Street Massacre," "Two for the Feast of Anthony the Hermit"; *Poetry:* "Ten Past Eleven"; *Poetry Northwest:* "A Colloquy of Silences," "In the Grotto of St. Euthymius," "Squirrels Worshipping Crows"; and *Quarterly West:* "A Guinness at Winkle's."

A fellowship from the National Endowment for the Arts and a leave of absence from Pittsburg State University helped the author begin work on this book. Its completion was aided by good counsel and support from several individuals, especially Gary V. Hartman, and Stephen Meats.

Contents

I am neither a prophet nor a prophet's son,
but a herdsman and a gatherer of wild figs.

Amos 7:14

The Minotaur

I find myself in the midst of the country
and I've lost my son. Where is he I ask
and someone I meet on the road says he saw him
day before yesterday in a culvert up the road.
All of a sudden a field of blighted corn
comes creaking by like a crowd of dead men
and an old tire says KEEP OUT BAD BULL
because they have him in there someplace hidden.

Afternoon with Angels

I was singing as if for my life. I hung
my lungs from the rafters and I sang them dry.
I made a blue light shine from them like a fire
the angels of the ceiling were dancing round.
I was glad to have them have this song of mine.
Fathers of us, O fiery rafter dancers,
I am aloud with honor and compassion.
I spin the circles circles are spun from.
Ask me directions. I'm the one that gives them.
They went on dancing, so I kept on singing
until my breath was stones and my tongue cinders
and the life I sang from was the afternoon
the angels dropped around me as they vanished
into my skin and back to the cold blue sky.

A Winter Walk

The clouds came down around his shoulders.
Blackbirds bit like fleas in an old coat
somebody wore once in a field of stubble
by a battleground his grandfather left alive.
A woman kept smiling in his mind
leaning from her balcony wrist to chin,
the wall behind her bristling with brothers.
New snow was falling. That was long ago.
The blackbirds drifted among cottonwoods
like snipers in old coats. She watched him
stop by the road, as if to think which way
his walk would take him. Making up his mind
he bent to pick up something under him.
And that was what she said it was like to her.

Pilgrimage

I was on my way to a holy place in Asia
to view the bones of Christ. Stopping to tie my shoe
I couldn't help listening to blackbirds
in a stand of hickories around a clearing.
I kicked some rocks to prove I had shoes on
and kept on walking. The sight of blackbirds
reminded me of my father's eyelids sealed shut,
his face as brazen as an emperor's.
It was a quiet day but for the blackbirds.
They cried in my mind while I knelt and prayed.
The bones of Christ were gold in a glowing coffin.
People had come from all over that country.
One side of Christ's face lay gazing at a window
through which one blackbird slid, carving the air.

~A Guinness at Winkle's

Before I started up to where the Oratory was
I spoke to Mrs Lynch about the lack of items on the menu.
The hurricane had sucked all the fish back to the ocean
and fish was all they would have in this shop she said.
On the shelves behind her were platters of sacred cake.
Outside, the Bay was breaker after breaker.
The roofs of Kinvara were white as milkmaids' bibs.
I said a Guinness at Winkle's Hotel would taste good
so I stepped down the street past the ruins of the Oratory.
Up through the ceiling among tiers of archangels
a great catalpa clawed the sky. I rumbled downstairs.
At the turnstile Father Abbot waved me through
to shanties by black water. I was nowhere
near Kinvara and a long way from where you were.

−Fathers

We talked to our Jamesons at closing time
about our fathers' last words. I said mine said,
Keep your nuts tight, meaning electric wire nuts,
and you said yours said, See you in April, boy.
Those were our two damn shames in Dublin that night.
We walked back and sang us a couple of damn shames.
I said I had drunk a little and felt good
and you said you were sober as you could be.
We tried to decide which was finer, the Champs
Elysées or O'Connell Street, but couldn't,
so we went to sleep discussing the fine points.
Out in the lamplight somebody kept yelling
to somebody else two or three blocks over
who yelled back once. It got quiet after that.

For Gibbons Ruark

The Windowsill

1

I thought I could tell them it was raining
in my body. There were lights on my limbs.
I held what I thought was my face into
what passed for air and I cried when I breathed
so loud you could hear me under water.
It was me or them. Some of you might know
what I meant by that. The longer I cried
the more it seemed I kept having reasons
to go on crying as loud as I could.
Some of you might tell me why this happens.
Anyway, I told them it was raining
inside me and the trees had lights in them
so I could find my way home in the dark
so I could blossom by the windowsill.

2

Leaping from eaves were droplets big as babies.
The world was blue. Even the roofs were all blue.
Blue were the baby droplets that fell from eaves
into everlasting watery ruin.
You would have said it wasn't that way at all,
that was nowhere near the way it was, I was
dead wrong. It was yellow outside. The drops fell
from the eavetroughs like acorns from the pin oaks
and I was badly mistaken. Oh, I said,
I am glad that you mention that, yes I am.
I am coming along all right in any case.
I wish I could pay you for the things you did
when I was needing a good kick in the face.
Already I am feeling a great deal more calm.

3

I watched and watched and tried to think and thought
about the way the birds came down the sky
so that I kept on wanting to know why
people like me were always getting caught
in front of God and everybody. What
else was I but my own worst enemy
dangerous to leave in my own custody
who should be put where all the doors were shut?
Slowly the girls came turning in their dream
among the waters where the fishes swam.
Some of them looked to see me. There I was,
lingering beside the littlest of them
watching the way she stood on that boy's knees
and dove and disappeared with the fishes.

4

All of the ways I spelt it it was not
good news. A kind of song dwelt in my mind
that said You may lie easy on that side,
but I kept thinking Maybe that's just it,
I hate to lie down overmuch, I get
this odd susceptibility to light
when I lie easy for too long. One time
when I was a boy I was knocked so flat
I couldn't see for two maybe three days
then gradually I saw lights and a face
and flowerpots swinging in the windows
and everyone bending with looks of grave
bewilderment, and I batting my eyes,
then someone remembering what my name was.

5

What I did was I looked up at them and I said
The best of you bend with the beating of the wind
that whistles between the living and the dead
and shuffles the lucky from the left-behind.
I wasn't in need of more than the way home
from any among you that might have lent
light enough on the subject so a damn
fool like me could make it even half bent.
After I said that I kept my mouth shut
and lay low. The next day I was a good
ways off and in the kind of place I thought
I would have been luckier the way things stood.
I tried to lie there most of that night until
the moonlight woke me from the windowsill.

6

I heard them talking. I could not get up.
A fiery beast was standing on my breastbone
while I kept trying to grab him by the top
of his head and pry him off me, but my one
good arm was feeble as an old lady's
so when I reached I reached into thin air
and grabbed at the father of all our bodies
whose face is a blazing glass where you disappear
from even your own sight and come on through
not exactly into what I would call light
but something like it in the way it drew
my eyes toward it. But then I was all eyes
spinning and spinning in the great eye of God,
constantly wondering what it was I did.

To the Wreakers of Havoc

When the wind blows in Kansas in springtime
the afternoons surround us with hosannas
brought into town by bands of the redeemed.
About their heads are halos of butterflies
and once they arrive in Applebury Mr. Mayor
awards them the freedom of the place and even
Jack Prettyman at the liquor store makes a buck
from the flush customers up and down Broadway.
Nobody minds what happens here. Every one
has the right idea. Better that blest Arapaho
pausing to marvel over watches and flatware
than a leader of men or seller of merchandise.
The Great White Father is a bad cadaver.
Step to one side of him. Get with the butterflies.

For Louis Postai

The Spring of '64

Whatever the reality, it is
a reality. The door isn't shut,
the door's open. That was Henry James's
word from a lady bound to die, but what
could be the least thing the matter with that
as a lifelong attitude? One evening
in the spring of '64 the sunset
broke from a cloudbank like a door opening
onto a golden room and a voice said
I am none other than the Living God,
and I remember how I was impressed
enough to go home that night filled with trust
in the way things seemed to be working out.
I hardly ever slept with the doors shut.

The Sea off Flanders

The seascape in that odd dream was the same one
Icarus keeps drowning by in the Brueghel,
complete with plowman and enchanted swain,
except, while I watched, a wayfaring seagull
fell down out of heaven to the doomed boy's foot
and settled its wings to gaze at that fat ship
that breasted the sunset. Before the bird could look
Icarus slid peaceably into the deep.
The gull had nothing but sea-foam to grab at
so it flapped back where it came from. Joachim
the farmer and Nicholas the idiot
both said they might like to go sailing sometime
to places no one ever dreamed of going to
where people could fly like that boy tried to do.

Squirrels Worshipping Crows

When we are dead
and our tails flick
in the street
what is left of us lights
in the high branches
where the thin twigs dangle.
Then we fly.
We find out what the fire
in the sky is like.
Leaping around in it
we become coals with wings.
Thousands of us perch
in the great tree
in the middle.

The Perfect Fool

I was in the land
of the bland and the raptureless.
I wasn't all there was
of the likes of me.
Doors hung limp on their hinges,
dogs sprawled in the sun.
Habitual words kept forming
in the light above houses
like captions in hunting scenes.
I grew tired and listless.
My feet kept moving.
One day the women all
came down to the sidewalks.
We stepped off arm in arm.

Father Finbarr Remembers the Major

Here is the picture of the three famous statues.
There was a flicker of bird-drift over the oakwood.
The light was ablaze but the cool of the day
had descended and we sat rubbing our sleeves.
The land was a sullen undulance on all sides
and the sheep came munching while their backs rose
to show there was some way to tell sheep from stones.
Often I think how the Major must have yearned
for the twilit lives of townsmen on a prowl
just after the bend of the road by the Great House.
She would be fussing over her comely supper
at the great oak table. Sunlight would bend
its blade in the doorway. On his way out
under the broadsword his forefather plied with Cromwell
the jackdaws would be diving through eyesockets massed
in ivy. He would lie by that ruined tower at Shanrahan
soon enough, where Father Paul tells how he came upon
a locket with yellow hair and a ring behind some mortar
in the wall above the graves of two young people
who drowned in the River Duag there beneath the bridge.
Tonight it would be June and birds and late sunfall.

Here is the photograph of Brother Berchmans and me
by the balustrade at Shanbally Castle. Count us.
I count three. The Major was off in Europe at that time.
It was during the Second War and we were visiting
with Mrs Quinlan who kept the gardens there. It was she
took this picture. Elizabeth is the woman
in the white raincoat. The sun had come out again
and I can remember a rainbow in the east meadow
that hung entirely from hedgerow to hedgerow.

Not long after, Shanbally was brought down stone by stone
and the Major had come home to dwell with Elizabeth
in the great townhouse at Clogheen. Once he was
out in the evening he could hear the birds.
There was a gleam that played on the west turret
as you came towards the Castle from the road
that would keep flashing in the back of his mind.
As he entered among his townsmen under dustbeams,
doffing that broad white hat you found him in that day,
for a time the face he gave them was a glad one.

— The Way West

I hitched a ride to Cork from Cappoquin
the evening of the thirtieth of May.
The man that drove me was a traveling man
with some sort of a garment company
so there were ladies' garments in the back
in boxes with all sorts of literature,
but after a dozen words we hardly spoke,
except around a few jars at Lismore
where we met Mickey Keane who said the Duke
that had the local castle was his cousin
in a small way, only he'd had the luck
and Mickey hadn't was the only reason.
I honestly believed him but we went
before I could find out if this was true.
I figured you could make up what you want
about yourself in this country somehow,
having it your way—nobody really cared—
and where was there the harm to anyone,
particularly if he called himself a lord
like that one that belonged to Mickey Keane?
We were almost in Cork about this time.
I decided that my friend had had a bad
experience of some kind that kept him mum,
so I got out at the first stop I could,
wished him good luck and walked up Merchants Quay
toward Patrick Street, the thirtieth of May.

Gifts

The message on my father's pocketknife
used to read Downriver Refrigeration
before the last white dab of it wore off.
He had calendars from Young Supply, pens
Geo. Johnston & Sons Air Conditioning
Sales & Service would give at Christmas, even
a plastic dashboard tray to put things in
from Westside Scrap Metal, including pens
and the pocketknife, which I inherited.
A shopkeeper in the Dodecanese
tried to swap me a beat-up Greek boy-scout knife
for my father's from Downriver, but I wouldn't.
I told him he could keep the knife. I gave him
a corncob pipe instead, which made him smile.
He said from now on when he smoked this pipe
he'd have his friend Mikális in his mouth.
So when I hold my father's pocketknife
I feel the thumb that used to give against
my palm when we shook hands. And we shake hands.

The Voice in the Rafters

I have gone down
into the place under the house.
It is damp there
and I keep thinking
that somewhere out of the shadows
someone is coming
to take me home.

I look for a way out.
Up in the rafters
as I begin to see them
is a skylight with sky in it
and birds and waving trees
in a world where green things move
against the blue.

I stay where I am. I pull up
a ring with a door in it
and I step down.
In the light over the table
my father's shadow is reeling.
His face looks toward me and he says
"Come here," but I don't come.

Then I turn around
and the light has a hole in it
with more light beyond
so I reach for it with both hands
raising my arms like a wild man
and the song I hear
is my own voice multiplied

so I go flying out
as the green things move
against the blue. No one else
is out there. It is just me.
I listen to what the song says
and it tells me "Go on,"
so I go.

Dreaming of Women

This never happens. You never get to look
at the insouciant blue above the garden
where a stone frog sits on his stone at the foot
of a woman whose rain-stained breasts are naked
as any real woman's one morning in bed,
grape-arbors ripening beyond the casements.
She'll never notice you taking this all in,
but the stone frog might, with that slap-happy grin
frogs normally don't wear. This is a fiction.
I wanted to talk about our awkwardness
as human beings—how, on account of it,
we sleep in Saturdays, dreaming of women
in houses with back rooms behind the back rooms.
One of them wants to walk out into the rain.

Grandmother

Sometimes I go back to where she is
leaning above the garden with its stems that look
like rhubarb sweetening the afternoon. The sky's
blue never lingers this way except in the back
of the part of my head I keep them in, the ones
I left there where she is. The sweat on her neck
chills her when she stoops and looks where the sun's
ambiguous forehead glances like the King's in that deck
of poker cards we played with. Her thumbs are spoons
dipping the dirt. She gathers her breath and prays:
Lord, make me brave to praise you for such luck
as I must learn to live with to the end of my days
evidently, thanks to your good grace. Some afternoons
she would talk like that. Often it got that black.

The Lives of the Just

At first it made me less than happy, this blunt
predicament I had been born to work in:
nightly I plundered my brains for an answer

and oddly enough answers would often come
in numberless guises, trooping around me,
grabbing my shirttails to get me to bend down

into my own goodly brains where they would dance
and holler in a wildness I was hard-pressed
to reckon with, I was that unused to it,

though I had dreamt it often and heard its cry
and watched it skulking fiercely in the bushes
back to its lair with that black look in its eyes

that told me *It is the likes of us that feed
on the likes of you, and once we scrape you clean
we go on starving* and stood me up in bed

most of the night that night, trying to throw off
the ones that scoured the bracken in full cry
cracking the air with hunger blacker than any.

For an Epiphany

Days like this in winter your mortality
weighs lighter, the thought of it doesn't pry
the backdoor of the soul so easily.

Go out in it, get loose in the great air.
Put off what makes you weary earlier
than usual and strive to say, I dare

you: I won't die today, I'm good for one
more, let it happen. Listen to the man:
he's giving sermons now. One afternoon

you'll find him on your doormat dressed to kill,
handing you a tincan in which a single
nickel clatters, and with a face so full

of radiance the tears start in your eyes
so you go searching for the five twenties
you hid in any number of mattresses.

You'd give him anything for word like that.
This is the parlor of the Infinite.
Come in. It's good to see you. Have a seat.

On Completing My 40th Year

I stepped inside the temple of my soul
one Saturday afternoon in the winter
and it was a bright place. There were some people
from Indiana there and I met their daughter
who was a homely skinny thing in spectacles
and we got talking about life in ancient Greece
and I kept thinking about how some Pericles
had gone to a good deal of trouble so this
oddly adorable creature and myself could carry on
over these bloodthirsty complacent stones
that kept a few lean shadows from the sun
like beggar children up among the ruins.
Then they were gone and night came on at once
and it got cold among the monuments.

The Last Great Lover

A man rows out to sea in a boat no bigger
than the extended arms of his life.
Lighter than balsa it wobbles over the waves.
The leathery box with his belongings
has lost its lid and flights of loveletters
erupt over his wake. He pauses a little
beyond sight of land and says his prayers.
The thought of some almighty emptiness arises
in the back of his mind while prayers like gulls
flock to that quiet place in the eye of the sea
which might be the eye of God for all he knows.
Then wonderful visions of women in towels
kneel to anoint him. He goes on rowing.
Out of his round red mouth pour songs of wooing.

Two for the Feast of Anthony the Hermit

Ora et labora

1

That sky, that all but shining place or thing
keeps up pretense of airy tedium
before the window I keep looking from
wondering where the birds went that would sing
with such wild gusts of crazy caroling
you'd think the wind was singing as it came
to blow the likes of us to Kingdom Come
out of the cold-front not a single wing
cut into on its way from Wichita.
What does a person want who looks and waits
for light to thrive on and for music too
from places further than his just deserts?
It must be desert places after all
that keep some listeners lonesome for snowfall.

2

Then we made love. It made me feel so good
I said to hell with all this gruesome crap
about the birds and hermits. I am fed up
with goose-step measures and a prim rhyme-scheme—
sweet bleeding Jesus I am tired of them.
Outside was January. It was cold—
enough to freeze the teardrops from men's eyes
and stand them staring like infernal trees
full of the spirits of the dead-for-good.
I know I said that more than once. That's good.
This little poem got lonely, so it said
Give me that good word that you got once more.
I'm glad to do it. That was awfully good.
The wood was singing in the bedroom door.

⌐The Miracle of the Nails

One day in mid-September when Saint Francis
was approaching 43, he received the Stigmata.
A hole in his side oozed blood. He needed
special socks to cover the wounds the nails
had made and kept on making in his feet
because these nails were actually nails
not just the prints of them, they were
hooks of iron under his soles. His hands
with the nails in them were torn and bandaged
and tucked up his sleeves so he only showed
the fingers. This went on until the day he died
and Francis sang because he was happy
and safe in the knowledge that he would gain
Heaven, which Pope Gregory said he did
so then Francis was a saint. I rode
my bicycle around town today thinking
about this. I kept my bare feet free
of the sprocket and I sang my song
to the humming of the tires. And I came home
to continue singing as if to the blue sky
where the roof left off and it was all blue
above the windows and the trees. As I bent
in blessing on my neighbors and my kinsmen
I practically bled all over the neighborhood.

The Blessing of the Bones

The blessed Enzo Schiappa rests under glass
in the duomo of Ozzodivenza in the Dolomites
and despite the snarl that is left of his face
and the fingers that look like broken bits
of kindling about to burst into flame
around the crucifix in the midst of them

people have reason to kneel in reverence
beside this rotten excuse for a saint.
His father was a minor poet from Florence
in Dante's time who once, for amusement,
cursed God in the presence of many and fell dead.
His mother was a shopgirl this man had impregnated.

Enzo grew to manhood with the Dominicans,
his mother having disappeared when he was small.
He joined the friary as one of their sacristans
and came to be much loved for his wonderful
jocular piety. At his death the chimes
he used to pull rang eighty-seven times

for the years of his life. When they went to find
who was ringing them, no one was there.
The ropes hung motionless. Local legend
maintains he was able to pray his father
out of Purgatory, despite that wretched sin.
People linger by his bones to be spoken clean.

A Feast in February

If I could tell the mankilling majesties
how I can hear a singing in my skin
from the way animals get around in daylight

squirrels in particular
from bush to pin oak
I would be mindful of that saint

who lost his unlikely head,
covered with cockleburrs, because a lady
happened among his beanrows and he rebuked her.

She brought the poor man to law
where he made known to them a point of view
not in accord with the official posture.

When they gave him his martyr's crown
it was February 23rd.
First there were crows then angels looking on.

Serenus in Heaven seventeen centuries
and me in Kansas trying to get word
from the lives of animals.

What I meant before was true.
I hear it. It sings to me in my sleep
and is always singing

like a boy by himself up an alley
someplace in the Baja
within sound of the sea.

The sun is a pinwheel in the middle of the sky.
Miguel the barber
draws down his shade for siesta.

Boats painted sky blue and blinding white
rock in the harbor
beside specks of sunlight.

Of Those Dear to Him

These daily graces, common decencies,
spun from the dingy business of the life
we keep on leading, by whatever means,
are, as in one of Yeats's best ideas,
measures appointed against disbelief,
boredom and bloodiness, for our children's
sakes especially. Once they have witnessed
an open window with a yellow bowl
beatified by the curtains' rise and fall
in bright September, some few things at least
come clear, as if, despite the dearth and dust
that flesh has coming, for a little while
the soul can traffic with the natural,
by dint of which the lot of us are blessed.

A Tale of Bears and the Blackbirds

Out in the moon the souls of wolves
are blue-gray candles in the woods
and nightbound blackbirds making moves
from limb to limb obey the gods
that glint from white leaves at the moon,
wide as a rowboat over weeds.
Or so he tells me. This goes on
all midnight long. The great bears come
and where there had been moon the sun
stipples the ground. The trees are calm.
More bears have gathered like old friends.
We listen and we hear them drum
beyond us in a crazy dance
while we lie quiet as we can
nudged among nettles, twigs and stones.
The blackbirds high above begin
from where they sit against the sky
to shake their rainy voices down.
At this I turn to ask him why
he told these things the way he did—
where the bears go, how he and I
come to be there, and why he said
blackbirds have voices like the rain.
Because I thought a blackbird would
if something in the air said rain,
he tells me. And it starts to rain.

Ten Past Eleven

This is the time of day the mailman comes.
This is the mailman who dreams every night
that his mother is home from vacation in the grave,
waiting to greet him in the kitchen in the sun.
He goes on down the sidewalk in his brisk black shoes.
All the homesick letters ever written are dangling
from the halltree in his brain. We are nowhere
near the ocean. There is sunlight everywhere.
Life has a curiosity undreamt of in other ages.
We dream in circles, answer our own loveletters,
stir soups all day in kitchens for the dead.
They primp in our mirrors, borrow our talcum powder,
and depart by way of the backyard picket fence.
This was the light we found ourselves in once
when everyone kept coming through the musty vestibule
on their way in to see us where we sat in the sun.

The Garden Party

It isn't so much the abundance as the surfeit
as when, by halflight, multitudes of dark birds
refuse to thin and drift in broken strands
but hang in great remorseless thunderheads
crackling with cries. Such hunger
nearly undoes us. Lingering where we do,
safe amid hedgerows bristling with persiflage,
you say it would be easy to vanish here.
The quaking patriarch in the gray gown will come
with cautionary grimace to lean by the wall,
hands tucked upsleeve while his eyes beckon
for which of us would go, and you would go, you say,
gayly into the maze. Once at the other end
good Guernseys lift their jaws from the greensward
oblivious in an oblivion of dragonflies. Crazy
without you, I shake my face from the balustrade.

Fourteen Sentences at Midwinter

The snow is general all over Kansas.
I climb to the attic for a look upstreet.
The great pin oak by the corner is half white.
One could be cold a long time in those branches.
The sky turns to iron and the tree blanches.
It is like the inside of a hermit's cave.
He sits in the mouth of it barely alive.
Suddenly he abandons himself to bliss.
That blackbird settling there in that elm is him.
In the ashram of the sun he sits and dreams.
One of his cousins comes and invades his light.
He takes off trailing ribbons of requiems.
Just after that it's the middle of the night.
I wake and stare at the dark for a long time.

A Colloquy of Silences

That calm above those trees in the gray spaces
among the crosswork of the twigs and branches
and thin birdwhistle piping into silence
with other further birds whistling in answer
among the selfsame silences. I answer:
we weren't meant to live among these spaces
except to scare our hearts out in the silence
that makes us wonder what the upper branches
of trees can have learned about the main branches
of wisdom and the sources of the answer
to the question about why all this silence
must persist among those elegant spaces
beyond the gray spaces around tree branches
where the silences of birds are the answer.

Midsummer Light as the Soul's Habitat

It wasn't the turnings of appearances
nor any of their exactions from the air
that made me think the afternoon was bees
or gangs of bears in rowdy robes of fur.
I hadn't thought of this for any reason
and this wasn't anyplace but my backyard.
Here was the flavor of an illusion
that stuck to my tongue like a hummingbird
beating its wings into a blur of hunger—
one of those tones from the soul's undergrowth
where animals devoid of any anger,
lifting up bits of landscape in their teeth,
would turn to look around them where they were,
loosening their faces into shreds of fire.

A Voyage to the Island

We sail there together. He resolves to stay.
I return home to marry and raise children.
My last son is a poet who, coming of age,
heads over to locate my old companion,
who long since, in the cool of his cave,
has come to satori. Up walks the last son,
seeking him out for what his father told him,
so he and the hermit set off for the hills
to receive certain visions. One afternoon
they witness the Buddha bending into himself
in the shape of a scorpion curling its tail
and eyeing them hour by hour amid the blazing day,
which drives them mad. Eventually they open a hotel.
I arrive for a visit, having failed at everything.

In the Grotto of St. Euthymius

It began in a house with something wrong with it,
falling bricks and bursting water from the ceiling.
She was trying to help me put my shoes on
for the long journey up Vernor Highway on my bike
toward the Holy Places on the East Side
where the smokestacks of Detroit Edison were minarets
and cripples sprawled their deflated legs on the sidewalks
begging endlessly for the end to come, for the light
to burst in us till we all glowed like lanterns.

It was 1965 in Paris on the Boul' Mich somehow,
sycamores in cages, whey-faced girls in white dresses
and next to the storefront with the Mont Blanc pens
an old woman in rags asleep on the sidewalk
with one palm upraised and a 5-centime piece in it
big as a badge that said Let me in, let me in, I'm with
the Ministry of the Poor, this is our dream.
You people can move along now and head on home
and leave us our dream. In the shadows of the sycamores

it was later on that day in the old neighborhood
in Detroit again. You wanted to argue that Mozart's brain
was no better than a fine machine, that not one of us
could exceed the capacity we started with. The point
was lost by the time we had turned up the alley
with the little grotto in it where the Saint looked out
from behind his windowpane heaped with wilted sprigs
and candle-ends and two of his own shinbones
and the ivory ring bestowed on him by the Pasha.

The Eighth Street Massacre

Early suppertime.
I step into the backyard.
The ground is yellow hands
applauding the cat and me.
We have come together
to sing our country's songs.

In the forgotten acres
under the sunflower's cracked
and terrible skeleton
the children of the poor
are scuffling in their chairs.
We have begun to sing.

Blackbirds leap from tree to tree
like shadows of partisans.
I step through the front door.
My father has brought guns.
We chase them up Eighth Street.
You keep laughing and calling me.

Jacob Limps Home over the River

Day broke after I strove against God's face.
I woke alive. The light grew in the trees
and last night's dream was all that bothered me—

the one about the nuns' mummies in coffins
at Mariners' Church where atheists came to pray.
A cup of coffee and a cigarette

took care of that. I didn't give a damn
what my dream said. There were a pair of squirrels
embracing the oaktree. Elderly Mrs. Kempster

was watching Brownie's stub wag in the bushes.
She had a keyring with a gleaming key
to guide her yard by yard. The old man stayed

away, he wasn't coming home, not this
old man. She'd never find him. He was gone
for good. The entire neighborhood had brightened

with April in the middle of February.
You can't go back again—that was the dream's
own turn of phrase—the one I woke up from

with cool knees in the hollows of my knees,
an arm over my breastbone, chin against my ear,
the morning coming on us from the street

loud in the window open to blue light
and mountains like gray cats. That was that August
in the Islands, in another life. The train

from Istanbul would come to take us home
through too much slivovitz in Slovenia,
the Simplon Pass at night, Paris by dawn,

a long talk on a bridge above the Seine.
Then in she walked to tell me it was time
to rise. Here it was morning, it was back

on Euclid Street, we only had each other.
The dark wind of the dream blew back to sea
and God was captain of the one ship home.

Stubb's Understanding
of Sun, Moon and Stars

Up in the heaven there were bright assassins
that plowed the deep with faces white as linen.
Somewhere inside me I fell into a sleep
where there were women strolling from door to door
up and down an alley off a narrow street
where I kept prowling like a crazy angel.
Next thing I knew I was in with one of them
and I could see her breasts smiling out at me
from above her petticoats that kept flying
up past her head like big sheets of heat lightning
and then her belly was beckoning at me
and I was in my stockings beckoning back.
It was no use. In the backyards of the sea
I was reaching for cherries, great ripe red ones.

Queequeg Wonders What He Means

Sometimes I look down when I am shaving
the back of my head and the two long
bands that run over my belly
are the twin rivers of the creation.
As I bend down they spill onto my ankles
and probably beyond them into the big well
I keep falling into for some reason.
Once I am looking long enough that way
I start to imagine what it must be like
in the place where the rivers empty.
Maybe the girls there lead you
up to their houses where the walls
are like the insides of big blossoms
with fat plums bursting open next to them.

Brown Socks

When she wears her brown socks
I want to get down and rub
my nose up and down her calves
and put my tongue under both knees
with a look on my face that says
Hopeless Case. When she takes off
the same brown socks I think
of the way the moon looks
on a cold cloudless night
over the backyard. I lift my face
in my two hands and lay it
above the trees. My mouth is
open wide and I am singing
like the last blackbird to head south.

Kathy Dancing

When she dances I think she loves herself
that much, she can leap for the joy of it,
she can whirl on her toes in her bare feet.
Sometimes I feel like singing when I think
of the way she raises her legs when she dances
and the look on her face when she sees me
watching her lift her legs when she dances.
I wish I could throw my voice up over the roof
to sing the praises of this lady and her feet.
I feel like unfurling my smile from my shoes
to my forehead and drifting off over her hair
that whirls around my face as I pass over her
looking down to find her dancing in circles
that keep growing wider and wider and wider.

The Parting Glass

Such honor as was done
to me and my good name
on account of the one
deed worthy of acclaim
that I did among them
could turn a man's heart grim
from wishing he had gone
and bid them to leave him
and his kinsmen alone
for no other reason
than that the hour had come
for some to be off home
adream in the one room
among the wife and son.

To Cathleen at Patricktide

> . . . I saw a young girl,
> and she had the walk of a queen.
>
> Yeats

If you'd come back I'd make a rime of it.
I'd say, It took you long enough. This place
got lonesome and then lonesomer night by night
until we all gave up, or almost did.
One of us stood and hollered at the moon
begging for nothing but the moon's regard,
but all that happened was the moon went down
and it got so dark that the man said, God,
there's nobody out here but me and stones
and hunger from some raging demiurge's
worst intentions toward the likes of me.
I'm going in before the cold comes on
and nighttime fills the middle of my bones
with fire's own opposite, the dearth of fire.
Then in he went, and nothing came about
out in the bogland where he said these things,
though nobody could show it to a child
or any simpler creature wanting comfort.
If you'd come back at such a time as that
I would have said the moon had taken form
and risen in the face of woman now
and given reason for the souls of men
to climb amongst a merriment of suns
bearing no burdens but the ones they love.

Other Titles in the Contemporary Poetry Series